WRDPLAY

lloyd owens

soulink publishing...

Text design by lloydowens/kleandesign

ISBN 978-1-300-05753-6

wordplay for foreplay.
wordplay for love's sake..
wordplay for your worst day...

in the end, words can be both heavy and light, they carry both life and death within them... #choosewisely

I know, I know, I know... This is where the Table of Contents would be, if there was one...

The truth is, I never wanted one. My desire was that you, the reader, would open the book and get lost in flipping from page to page to page. It's my hope, that wherever you choose to peruse these pages, you are compelled to keep reading, rereading, smiling, laughing, and allowing the words to woo you and your spouse or that special someone in your life.

These words are now your words. Wordplay now belongs to you. Have fun, fall in love, rekindle a flame that has become a memory, rediscover love and share.

So now that you are here... go ahead, turn the page and find yourself getting lost in love...

DEDICATION_

this is for love, for the lovers of love, for those haunted and tormented by what they thought was love... this is for those who want to RElearn love... this is for #her

W♥RDPLAY

I've waited...
For the right moment... the right time.
The words to fall from beneath the lips of clouds, like your
smile...

Lipstick lingers
Scented pillows
Forbidden thoughts due to previous commitments
Wishful thinking tainted by lust filled wishing
Treading water…
Wanting of another chance to create new memories
Passionate glances and fairy tale endings of blended families
I can dream of holding hands
Being the reason you smile
And being your man...
…It never hurts to dream

Sunlight peaks through blinds to find two souls limp, twisted into one, as the sun's fingertips trip through last night's passion...

In unison, the tandem escapes the clutches of warmth from the sun's caress,
                    Rolling into a new position, still one
with precision, they find themselves kissing the lips of
                    lust filled dreams...

At it again...
#themorningafter

Today I held forever in my arms
I can still smell the essence of her
I can tell she fell... fell for me even if only for a few
The morning dew that cascade between my fingers lingers
...she fit perfectly in my arms
Her skin soft
my fingers pleased
The small of her back I teased
An apparition maybe
Two strangers touching in such a provocative manner, yet needs
were met
I left before she could see my face, just before she came
An embrace unlike anything I've ever known
A wordless tongue lashing
Bodies dancing
Short lived but ever-lasting
Impressions left life changing
I was there but I wasn't there
No one's watching
No one cares
Or at least that's the lie she and I chose to believe...
In this web we so artfully weave with words & cold shoulders...
Yet, I'd hold her again if given a chance

Internal combustion
Mind wondering
Heart pumping
No confusion in love & lusting
At the same damn time
For the same damn mind
That belongs to a queen
Heat rising as nature stands
Towering, leaving everything else hidden in its shadow
It's the simple pleasures…
Like forehead kisses
Undiscovered soaked treasure
That lead me, no carrot needed, to the conclusion
That how I'm feeling is no delusion
And I'm head over heels…
Her heels over my head…
In love with you

Simple pleasures…

The treasure of her scent lingers, her smile pressed against mine…

My fingers soaked in her love's nectar, candlelight bubbles and wine…

… pleasuring her simply

Grace drips from your lips
Love dances in her eyes
Her smile shares wisdom without words
Her voice echoes through the chambers of my heart...
A fresh start...clean slate just in the nick of time
I know love...

She not only fits perfectly in my arms, but...
Her skin...soft, my finger tips...sprung
You see I wasn't looking...
To busy dreaming of bigger things
And it would seem that I dreamed her here right now...

floating in on a cloud

Trumpets blaring, His voice declaring, He is well pleased
So be at ease... and rest in this part of the journey...

I now know love and she looks just like you

WITH ONE WHISPER FROM YOUR LIPS,

I've come unglued
Ready to pursue with reckless abandon…love's morning dew
That nourishes from within
I'm listening for clues to woo & transcend
Lovers lost and sorrow filled blues…
Keys to unlock the treasures within your soul, that's adored in
perfection's light
Your voice, that catalyst of my dreams fulfilled
Your eyes, the ebb of my soul's waves crashing against the shores
of life...

{caught up in your light}

i've seen
the light
it's in
your smile
changed my
life...
forever

like king
i too
dream of
simple things
including us
exchanging...
rings

the first
shall be
last and
the last
shall be
first our
first kiss
our last
and last
names change...
bliss

Love's lipstick lay limp
As its message on my bedroom mirror… in bright red
Said something about...

"Wrong place, wrong time…
It wasn't you, but it's me"

Tempted to kiss the day dreams of you, that wrestle with my reasoning and dance with my desire...

...Apparition

I've dreamed this nightmare a thousand times
Cried until streams seem to fill up to the banks of my heartache
The damn has broken and flood waters rise
The tide in has washed away memories of heavenly engagement
Two souls, one rhythm, hidden treasures untold…COLD
Cold as ice…
She left me sitting at the edge of forever
Or at least that's what I thought the sign said
But I guess never was where she left me
Glad she's gone? Yeah
Because I've met a new shade of lipstick…a new treasure
She's sick, sicker than the bubonic
High… I'm on it… I mean Hi I'm lloyd
WHAT'S YOUR NAME?

Wondering if your eyes were really closed as we shared our first kiss

were the climactic treasures that seemed buried beneath your ugly past, real or mem-or-ex

your ex and axes fit in closets behind today's thrifting

I swore we lifted each other above the trash, the ash and the noise of our present condition

I can still taste your lips,
feel the warmth of you all wrapped around my everything

I can still hear your thoughts singing of pleasure filled pleasing

... seemed so real

Let me hold your hand
Kiss your soul
Let's crush our fears
Quench love's thirst
Embrace time's awful reflection
And paint new vivid masterpieces of dreamscapes

Where calla lilies grow beyond our reach
And the water is still our very own place of peace
Let's dance across rainbows
Our love the pot of gold… never ending
Where His voice echoes
Leading and providing for you, me... For US
Take my hand, close your eyes
Trust Him in me
Go ahead…it's safe to believe

sometimes...
i smile and laugh so you don't see me choke or choking on the
tears that live inside my eyes

sometimes...
i protest and confess security in being alone
but you see me curled up, fetal position, wishin' she was holding
me

sometimes...
sometimes... sometimes i hide...
but this isn't one of those times

i remember the sound of your voice
the taste of your lips
the warmth of your kiss
the words, glances and exchanges as we reached the peak
i remember the look in your eyes
i remember making love to you

hesitant but willing
    fearful yet longing
        ready but unsure
            wanting but controlled
                lusting but loving
                    all that is you...

if ever there was a heaven, i found it in your smile
the dance between words that are conjured up at the thought of
you the day dreams of things we'd do…

from first dates, to dances in the rain
to hand holding and sun sets, laughter til there's pain
from stories, to romantic get-aways
catching your tears and wiping away yesterdays
i'd live just to see your smile again
to know your deepest fears, your boldest dreams
i'd give almost anything...

i'm planning on this ending with a ring...

to symbolize heaven on earth and an answer to our dreams

whimsical whispers
turned into seductive shivers
from your ear lobe to your soul
to the wetness that lingers
your eyes demand more of what i have in store
forever isn't long enough to spend with you
my dreams span lifetimes with and inside of you
at the edge of tomorrow is so much promise
potential never looked so good
in this love, there lives no fear
just warm nights
perfect love candlelight
early morning lovin'
no more struggling
just you and me
from friends to lovers to forever's end

… i want you

morning kisses from your lips to the inside of your hips dripping wet, nothing left, bodies spent and it's only 7:45 in the morning

... can't wait for lunch

dim lit lights dance at ocean's edge   i beg for a chance to
envelope my lips with yours   an encounter to devour the soul
that lives within you   a chance to hold hands with an angelic
creature, whose stature embellishes the lines between reality and
dream sequences from your favorite movie   a groupie i've
become… she's the one   if not, i'll be done and alone…

your smile

i'd give anything to wake up next to your smile...

kiss you goodnight

my daydreams have grown wings and taken flight...

a plight i so kindly welcome

these thoughts, my pillow, a sweet rest

knowing that i've bumped into heaven's best

even if just for a this moment forever's indelible ink has left its mark on my chest, where my heart once lived

...can't wait to see what tomorrow brings

even your shadow heals my soul, satiates my desires and dances with me...

instantly tempted to undress your soul
hold your hands above your head

led by the sounds of love making
then taking you places you've only dreamed about
your imagination…

my playground no limits, no boundaries…

as lust filled whispers abound
tender tongue lashings caress every inch of you at this moment,
time stands still as i insert my will in your heavenly dew

exhausted we lay under a ceiling of stars the night sky…

our audience like them, i'm waiting for an encore

spent.
awake. drenched from wrestling with you in my dreams,
        skin to skin, my lips pressed against yours, we wrestled
lunging. challenging each to new climactic heights
reminiscing. laying in bed awake, wanting to go back to sleep to
meet you there devour. naked mental gymnastics
love.

forehead kisses
staring competitions
pillow fights at midnight
breakfast in bed
exchanging glances from across the room
picnics in the middle of nowhere.

i dare you to deny love! i'm patient. i'll wait for you to see. know
and see that we're everything we dreamed we'd be.

tiptoeing
thru
two
lips
her smile
lit the shadow covered room
as i
encouraged
her
flowers to bloom
        with
gentle kisses
that turned
to a
tongue lashing and nibbling
her eyes
danced
in the back
of her head
as she erupted
…morning love.

from a distance, i've chosen to watch the angels dance at the moments you smile. the night air longs to wrap itself up in you and i've dreamed of owning the hand that fits securely in yours. with an innocent persistence, i venture to risk it all to know you; to dance under moonlit skies with you; to create new daydreams of things with you; just the beginning of endless possibility and chances, where romance trust truth and love lives; where selfless giving never ends; where your smile lights the world "we" live in.

the sweetest dreams are those that begin with thoughts of kissing you and end with waking in you...

us...
simply stated, satiated, seductively sauntering thru memories of climaxes new. where, clinched fingers left indelible impressions in the air, just above our sweat ridden shadows that dance. oh how they danced to rhythms as simple as boom-bap, boom-bap, then a clap, a smack...the intensity of the melody's chant. explicatives i dare not mention, yet the tension could be seen in the stillness of us...our space, exploding together, patience's reward.

i am...
sick of yesterdays and her sun's rays, so i hide even from myself
within my skin
i run for solace's playground
i used to be the class clown
from tomboy to a tomboy's dream
i married seduction and divorced sanity
empty i lay here, legs crossed, one in today and out the other
smothered in yesterday's grey sullen distant memory
... i am

and i'm also alone

hopeless romantic
i lay frantic
trying to pace myself
thoughts of your smile invade my rest
leaving me tossing and turning…
wanting to pour out my heart
a fresh start for us both...
no past
no hurt
no pain
i would
if i could
make it all go away
leaving only the feelings that would allow us a chance to dance
in the rain...
two art lovers
creating art with words from our heart

with one glance
a million years ago i fell

fell like a star from out of a calm night's sky
i've dreamt you real from vision,
to an existence that stands before me…
heavenly your smile…

heart ready for love
perfect timing
perfect gift
finding you this you, me, us…

bliss

windless night my breeze…
your smile clouds seem to saunter past the stars
hoping to get their attention, like you have mine
the moon sits stoic arresting the thoughts of those that take time
to see him i see you and know you see me
the trees…
tall, gallant, even majestic
stand anchored, outlining a path to the rivers edge
hand in hand we tiptoe through the shadows of those trees
our protection as we approach a paradise unknown to either of us
the beginning of forever, the end of nowhere and the climax of
our journey at rivers edge, waters warm, vulnerable and naked
we dive in

in your eyes i've found my reflection…

timeless your treasure…

longing to be the pleasure that you've dreamed of holding you in
my mind your heart, my hands, your kiss…i've got plans
memorize my touch know the rush as my breath dance across
your body's length i'm focused…

certain that pleasing you has become my priority

if i mentioned the lust dripping from my lips or the way i long for your kiss this very moment i'd lay down my life for a chance at 3 wishes the first two would end with forever and you the last would be a chance for us to ask for more wishes let's explore the un-witnessed eternity's bliss the crisp sharp dagger of winter's morning breath where mountains and trees stand guard the trickle of streams seem to linger, wandering indoors let's dance to the rhythmic chants of snow flakes falling on the tin roof our skin lighting the fire for tonight...

if i mentioned this in a whisper or shouting in all caps, would you come with me?

… my first wish

vulnerable...

she lay across clouds blowing kisses to stars
the moon, her pillow at dawn she straddles space as her love or-
bits planets enveloped in her milky way...
her smile...

a second sun her eyes...
like the horizon telling tales of where she's been and where she's
goingher name...

timeless and it seems she's been looking and waiting for me
an astronaut with no shuttle, grounded
left longing for her

... my ms. universe

forever
reminds me of you
your smile
your curves
my world
your heart's song
music to my ears
caught up
i cease to resist loneliness…
cease to exist
this is no tryst
no frolicking
this ish is real
as real as it gets
infatuation grown up
with each passing moment
i own up to this feeling
accepting this responsibility
wrapped up in your arms
this…
this is what forever looks like… you remind me of forever

tracing your lips with mine
waking you
          sublime
suggestions erect erections
showing love's commitment in an instant
as moments pass
                    an inferno quenched time bent in our favor
dreaming…
i awake to simply savor all that is you my bright and new
forever… morning love

lillies dance in her shadow like a cool autumn breeze
radiant, delicate and simple is her treasure
her smile, a glance in her eyes
i've lost my way...
she like a guiding star
a breath of fresh air
an answered prayer
a dream's hopeful romance...
#uberspecial

lifeless, limp, lazy…
lay my love until she blew the breath of life into it rigid, robust,
rising…
            roars my love
        she gave it life
now we live...

two shooting stars take flight
chasing different dreams
vanishing somewhere between here and there
hoping to catch a glimpse of the others' trail
only to get turned around and crash into one another
creating a new future
new dreams
… hurry make a wish

the thought of your lips fully dressed in mine

a last first kiss

your hand surrenders as my fingers wrap around your grip…

next your hips

as we undress each others minds with our eyes words left
unspoken as our hearts whisper and our souls listen

we dance, our bodies one...
our last first kiss
led to this…
… bliss

love is... the ultimate sacrifice of self...

dancing
with her
shadow
her scent
dances in
the thin night air
holding her
so close
a dose
of forever lingers…

i'm healed
layers
pealed away
an angelic
display
of what's to come
i'm ready
for love
when you're
done
figuring out
if i'm
him
or not...

with love's lips
i tip toe through her tulips
get it…two - lips
skinny dippin'…
her waters crash upon my sandy beach
high tide…
a sip from her fountain gives me life

hapless affection

    led to

transforming sessions of whispers, gentle nudgings and love taps
as she wrapped her love round me and…"and suddenly" turned
into forever

enticing advances
chances for second glances
and encounters enhanced
by romance, lust and passion
an answer to lonely nights
and bad dreams
because… this thing is brand new
as the morning dew
everyday quenching
the thirst of wild flowers
to devour you…i'd give it all up everyday…
… for forever

forehead kisses
    just because
racing doubt in a hooptie
my life consumed by
could be, should be, and potential's distant cousin… would be

losing, but gaining on him
i let it all go finding hope
as the scene blurs to my right and left
my best foot pressing the pedal to the medal
silver and gold… i have none
when suddenly life came to a screeching halt
words flow, doubt lost
found love in an abandoned heart
empty yet filled with tears

    it's raining
as the tears came pouring out
to believe in myself sang the crowd
was all i needed to defeat the doubts

the outward expression of my love
left an impression only to be missed by most
a cost i'd surely pay again
to bend time and it's internal clock
wanting it to stop as our lips met
even if only in our subconscious space
a kiss i'll never forget…

wet were the lips that i kissed
holding your hips to savor
then devour a taste so sweet
a kiss that should last a lifetime…

even if only in my mind

… patiently waiting for you to believe

your world
my addiction
an old rendition of affection
my attention you own
perfection… i'm hooked

will broken… you took
my last, my best
nothing left
way too much for me
no remedy
no getting away soul lost
heart turned inside out
i'm lost unless holding your hand
your number one fan

your world is my addiction
an affliction i welcome
serving my fix…
your smile
selfless, i spend a lifetime
chasing this high
chasing the dragon…
that look in your eyes

i wonder...
what
where
we, you and i
could be, have been
had i just...
picked up my phone to call
to say hello
to ask you out
to check on your day on you...

i sit here, mind twisted, wandering staring at you
knowing that
you are special
beautiful,
intelligent
a wife in the making

                       ready

to be claimed

allow me the pleasure to discover a treasure thought lost and ill fated... at any cost

mentioning her name to Him
in every prayer, i wonder if He's told her my name… or that i've
been longing to look in her eyes, or that our purpose is
intertwined. I pray that her days are well, her nights peaceful and
her dreams real. I wonder if he's told her my name. As he guides
my steps, we prepare to cross paths. Will it be a smile or hello
that begins answered prayers?
I sit, pray and ponder… has He told her my name?

a genius in my dreams
orchestrating sunsets with one glance in your direction
tides rising, waves crashing
as my moonlight dances over your body
the breezes for fingertips trace the stars in your night's sky
lost in your eyes… an island whose treasure is buried deep
but i reach,
                    thrusting with the weight of pleasure
on my shoulders and hips a genius in my dreams…

refusing to wake up

imagine this
forever's bliss
fills the remnant vacancy left
by theft
of trust broken, guilt, hurt and shame
who knew that an angel was in my presence
delicate…
her flower, her heart, her smile
perfect for me
her heart, her smile, her dreams
heavenly…
i now sit at the edge of tomorrow's cloud
daydreaming of another chance
…another chance to dance
with her
hold her close
designed by Him for me
who knew that angels danced
with someone like me

darkness doesn't stand a chance in your light...

heaven
sent
with
one
kiss
with
these
words
fate
sealed
you
in
my
arms
{safe}
from
harm
two
previously
acquainted
strangers

my arms secure your legs i'm fed til' i'm full
your eyes…the back of your head

you said lead so i led, you to bliss' front door, love spell...

as the rain falls

i fall

the ground catches you with open arms but who will catch me
clouds move on the rain is gone yet i'm still

falling for you

i'll dream till you're real
till you're here by my side
done hiding… i'm searching
through the rubble of my past
through future unrest
for heavens best

for me…

for the angel whose smile fills my lungs and gives me life

… the perfect compliment

hanging on by a thread
i bled until there was nothing left
my best i'd give til' infinity broke and came to an end
till horizons choked and left only the wind
to see and feel…
waiting for love's permission to love again and win
so i spit fire through my pen
until then…

praying you will see
see my smoke signal

in the end, love's leftovers are discovered to reveal the truth
i'm your boaz
you're my ruth
yet being addicted to instant gratification
has left you with withdrawals of lovers
past and broken lust filled day-mares
and filled with empty feelings...
i wasn't prepared for this

instantly this position reminds of a fall breeze
as the wind caresses the length of her body...my kisses
this is the one that becomes undone
swiftly i fall into an abyss
lashings from lipsticks tip
trip me up as i drift off with the wind
like tree tops flopping back and forth
relaxing her hips
this is the one where stairs seem scarce
although i'm climbing her body
high knee... high knee
spent bent over
we rush down
until there's nothing left

i've dreamed about her all my life...

tonight, i trace the impression left by her hair on my pillow

stare at the hallway listening to her footsteps as she walks away

i can still feel her heart beating against my chest

i can feel her smooth skin on my fingertips

her kiss i taste...sweet as candy

her perfume dances for me across my room

time stood still...no seconds, minutes or hours past

i close my eyes to pray for her safe return

wondering if i'll ever find love, find her, again

... still dreaming about her

in her eyes...
horizons long
and towers stand firm
the dew on her petals,
wet from morning love
as glances turn to
second chances
breakfast fit for a king,
dessert...his queen

in her eyes...
a longing
thirsting
yearning
burning
for tender touches
and sweet whispers
pillow talk after tongue lashings
as the sounds of waves crashing
fill the night sky
that sits empty
...a voyeur into my dreams

kiss the lips of her sunshine at dawn at the edge of her wondrous waterfall cascading from the tip of her fountain surrendering to sounds of her pleasure and nature's treasure we rest...
only for me to wake her again

i wanna meet her and not regret a minute, moment, day or year

if i could rewind time
and it stood still, like tulips with no breeze...
beautiful
no interruptions
nothing to prove
i'd take it back to the first time i touched your hand
held your face
kissed your lips
the first time i saw you... all of you
before we ran in different directions
made alternate selections
choosing safe
this place we now find ourselves in
a pit
a cave
a tunnel with no light
until you show up again
unfinished
unrendered
undone
unmended
i've become the one who dreams about you... us... we
the love i can't release the music in my head
that i don't want to end
... that's you

hopeful romantic
dances for a chance to find love's lost hand
kept from being windswept as rain falls

washing away the tears' leftover stains
music drowns out the noise of loneliness' drums
that bang chaotic clumsy notes of discord

...looking for love

sometimes in silence

i can hear
her heartbeat
feel the
fluttering of her eyelashes
or her pinky toe
land on the floor
as she gracefully
saunters thru my imagination
…to know her is to know love

from
a
drizzle

to a downpour

crashing
waves
a
             tumultuous sea

fathoms deep

             i dove in head first

whimsically i whisper

wanton words of

willingness wonder and

wishful worlds with

(the) woman whose

wholeness withstands

waves wandering and

withholding what would

empty dreams
of scenes
reminiscent
of lovers wrestling
serenading winds
tiptoe through
open windows
and wanders
in between
the crevices
of our skin's connection
perfection
as the rain
flings itself
to the window panes edge
pledging to
catch a
glimpse of
our shadows
dancing on the wall

… mental stimulation

with precision i envision a night filled with cloudless skies and stars dancing to our rhythm, as we give them something to hold on to a voyeur's dream, as we collide to our own beat your sighs and moans...

the melody a picnic at midnight...you're my feast my dream come true my desire fulfilled my thirst quenched as your love dangles from...my lips, my hands, your hips...

with one kiss i see fields of flowers and rolling hills i've escaped yesterday and right now is overwhelming me with pleasures untold...

bold was our decision to create this song in the middle of a field untitled for now, but it's magic is sweet swept off your feet and in my arms we become one...over... and over... and over... and over

with my fingertips i trace forever's constellation across your body let them watch let them stare oblivious to everything, my attention paid only to you...

your eyes, your lips, your scent, your kiss the warmth of your breath against my neck...two bodies colliding creating music unheard percussion & melodies unsung...

hoping this night never has to end

love's language
languishes on
the serif of "elle"
the purest form

reborn

speech erratic
at best
silently i profess
through written word…
my thoughts
my chest pounds
with anticipation
              awaiting love's (that's what i call her) next move
as cotton candy
clouds in hues of blues sung by nina
parade down the halls of my mind…
to good to be true angelic in nature i, in lieu of distance
              I am persistent in returning "her touch"

… even if only in my head

words can contain the insane nature of this emotional adventure
or the chance i'm willing to take to fall in love with her words, her
smile, her hurts, her laugh, her voice
… even if only in my head

you're my feast
my dream come true
my desire fulfilled
my thirst quenched
as your love dangles
from my lips
my hands
your hips
with one kiss
i see fields of flowers and rolling hills i've escaped yesterday
and right now is overwhelming me

singing...
i'm searching for a real love...

a real love
as i reach
for empty sheets
her scent
is the only thing left
that holds me
drowning in the
streams that cascade down my face
haunted by...
by her voice that echoes from dark corners

i miss her...and we've never actually met

her touch...
her touch made me clutch the sky
made the heavens hush
yet in this deep still silence
i heard her heartbeat singing a song to me
damn… her touch

her touch...
more than a blush beyond a gush
my reaction attracted the attention of flood waters
as they rushed to see who summoned them
damn… her touch

her touch...
discombobulated
i felt obligated
to be still, to be free, to be
uncharted emotional highs
no lows soaring
i flew for the first time
damn… her touch

i've never really felt her touch
but as i day dream about that moment
that moment i've longed for all my life
… this is what i come up with

her locs draped over
    the mountains peak like fog
        i blew them to the side for a better view
breathless her valley screamed for me as i
stood in awe of her   w i n g s p a n

                               i... erect

began to climb as if my life depended on it
heaven sent
to the top i went
kissed her ink
on my way up
            lifted...

i've never been this high

at the edge of tomorrow
the seconds passing
looking back i hear her asking with her eyes for more...
another flight
another dance
a chance to pierce silence's heart
with pleasure's dart
a chance to wrestle
with climaxes
might she reach for me?
soaring we rode
never looking down...afraid of heights
simple pleasures, her eyes spoke volumes
...i listened

invisible
love
letters
line
the night's sky
like clouds
each written to her with my heart's pen
from stranger to friend
to dream filled
nights of holding hands
intimate whispers
and full bodied kisses
invisible moments
in my dreams again

simple
softness
under
my
fingertips
tracing
the
outlines
of
her
lips,
teasing
her
smile
wallowing
in
her
sunshine
dancing
in
her
rain

filling my cup, your love's nectar…honeydew flavored
falls from your lips to mine… a taste i devour slipping your jewel
between my teeth, caressing until it storms... the sky opens up
the thunder roars and we lay touching stars… drenched

in the midst of beautiful, i found you…
tracing your smile with my fingertips
i'm smitten… intoxicated
wanting to know your every thought… your every fear
to cover you in prayer
to cloak you in love
to dance in the rain
shameless i press forward to capture your every thought…
intention
let me be the decision you never regret
let me be him…
let me be your knight in shining armor
your night and morning
let me be him...
can i?

in the midst of beautiful, i'd find you…
tranquil, individual, potent
material for forever
daydreams and visions galore
i adore… you
your smile
the thought of your lips
every kiss
your swaying hips
lost in you
i wake every morning
my heart for you

if
given a chance to kiss your soul
i'll hold on to that moment forever
make love to your mind
dance in the rain until time... stood still

if
given a chance
i'd be the reason you smile
hold your hand
gaze into your eyes
whisper how beautiful you are
after kissing your cheek
nothing would matter
no need to sleep
because if given this chance
i'd be living my dream

in the morning
my thoughts are of you
your smile
your hands
your eyes
i stand longing for a glimpse…

a view

i daydream of tomorrows and forever
quenching our thirst for loves triumph
i stand
looking
longing
waiting
… for you

whether your
voice or smile
your heart or passion
i long to sit at the edge of your bed
listening to the thunder roll
the rain keeps pace with my heart's drum
as i come closer…
closer to you
your heart
your love
dreaming of kissing your smile
holding your hand
picnics and candlelit dinners

i dream of you...

in my dreams…
we lay skin to skin
my heart beats for yours

in my dreams…
my lips trace your curves
tiptoes through the ocean

in my dreams…
you are mine
and i am yours
forever has begun
as we become one

in my dreams…
love dances with lust
as we burst into heavenly heights
never landing
because you are in my dreams
…i never want to wake

tender
        moments make memories
in other worlds
as we tap dance
through constellations
        you ginger
        i'm fred
led by our hearts yearning
our loins burning
passion personified
as we picnic on clouds
your head in my chest

the thunder rolls in appreciation of our love

… conquest

addicted to all that is you…
lips
eyes
my hands
your hips
swaying to unheard before melodies and rhythms

drum beats…
our hearts in sync from the start
a pace unmatched by love's lust
trust offered and taken
but never taken advantage of
two become one
as we daydream of things undone
… like belts, hair in bra straps
love taps morph into tongue lashing

colliding…
sliding me between you
dividing only to be together
adding to what we already have

unspoken…
deaf and mute
i'd still be able to express
my love, my lust, my passion, my need of you…

for you
as my thoughts elope with yours
my heart saunters down the aisle with yours
picnics and shindigs replace lonely nights and emptiness
my words for yours
my heart is yours
my hand holds yours
as i devour
you quench
satiate
annihilate
your hunger
your thirst
matrimony of love bursts
fill my cup until it overflows
up up and away
cloud dancing
romantic gestures
and moonlit strolls
losing… lost any control
the beginning of forever
the end of never
as we become one...

with one glance
i seized a chance
a chance of a lifetime
to come close as ever
to placing my lips against hers... an angel

now thoughts dangle in my head of her lips
that kiss, the next taste of heaven
her in my arms, i dare not allow my thoughts run any further
to what the rest of her feels like under my fingertips
and her body's reaction
to my lips dancing
across her soft skin... heavens next

my lips, your lips...
my fingertips glide across your hips...

to be continued...

allow me to wrap my words around you... erasing yesterday, withholding nothing, exposing truths and finding forever

traveling for
miles with miles
jazz notes give me hope on this coltrane
headed to lovers lane
to your arms
and wet nights
under low lights
and cloudless skies
… can't wait to touch you

If missing was missing, would we miss her or even know she was missing? Maybe she was never here and what's missing is my dream, my lust, my passion…missed opportunity, as i missed my calling, missed the mark, missing my love and missing myself

heavenly position
intention's vision
a dream come true

no longer wishin'
or sittin' on clouds ledge
content with my decision
to sweep you off your feet
and dance a new dance
… an eternal retreat

paint my face with your love my hands firm grip
as i sip from nature's fountain an abstract rendering...
a work of art

love's script...
it's in braille

allow your fingertips to trace its infallible nature
with each impression... direction
leading you, guiding you

there are bumps and flat lines, peaks and valleys
each with a distinct purpose
no surface to rigid
too cold to bend and heat under the tips of your fingers
your hands hold the key, slowly opening a door that only
appeared closed
a soft landing for your fall
arms built for this
chest made to be the saddle for your locs
heart leaping with glee
in deed and in word... i am ready

love's
lipstick
left
an
impression
at
the
head
of
my
bed
reminding me of
what's to
come
tonight...

morning love…
it's morning love that's got me wide awake
a skip in my step
air under my feet
these moments are forever
this love, an endeavor
even if i was alone with just my thoughts of you
… good morning love

a shadow dances on the ceiling

to the rhythm of candlelight and heartbeats

pulse rising

breathing shallow

subliminal messages haunt the room

...the workout

intentional in
my mission
from this position
i peer into your eyes
trace your smile with my lips
cradled by your hips
...jazzy's song

from a distance
an instant seemed like forever
a smile
a kiss
then briskly whisked away to a lover's end

... my life

i've never been so close to the stars, as i am when i lose myself in
your smile...

instant submission had me wishin' this night would never end
or that i could bend time in my favor, to savor the moment you
said hello

wondrous water falls
falling endlessly to my lips
i sip from your cup/fountain
stars gaze in amazement of love created
the wind… our cover
the moonlight… the third lover
timeless, enchanting, panting…wanting for more
heights soared… unattainable until now
the end in sight
the plight of two spent souls who've become one
finished, but not done….
this is the beginning of forever

for 8,400 days i've dreamt the same dream
for 23 years dreamt the same name
as your mane lay across my chest
lost in our charcoal abyss
a simple kiss on your forehead
reminiscent of a rib lost
yet a woman gained
our heartbeat syncopated
love's exasperated and breathless
as my thunder, your lightening fills the air
soaked in your rain, my earth sips the cool waters
an eternal birth, perfection in our storm, heaven in your eyes
i'd dream this dream a lifetime

the end...

you sure you dont want to go back and read it again?